BE · AN · EXPERT

ENVIRONMENTALIST

JOHN STIDWORTHY

GLOUCESTER PRESS

London · New York · Toronto · Sydney

333

© Aladdin Books Ltd 1992
All rights reserved

Designed and produced by
NW Books Ltd
28 Percy St
London
W1P 9FF

First published in Great
Britain in 1992
by Gloucester Press
96 Leonard Street
London EC2A 4RH

ISBN 0-7490-0757-2

Design David West
Children's Book Design
Editors Catherine Warren,
Michael Flaherty
Designer Stephen
Woosnam-Savage
Illustrators Alex Pang,
Mike Saunders, Guy Smith,
Aziz Khan
Researcher Emma Krikler
Consultant Brian Price

A CIP catalogue record for
this book is available from
the British Library

Printed in Belgium

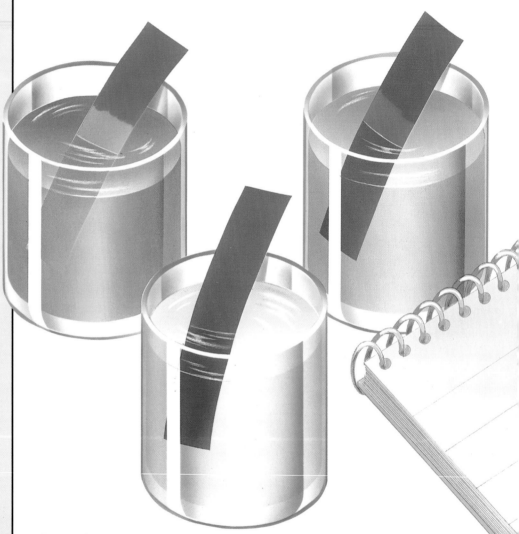

Photocredits
Pages 4, 12, 25 and 29 left: Robert Harding
Picture Library; pages 5 and 6 bottom:
Planet Earth Pictures; pages 6 top and 18:
Bruce Coleman Limited; pages 8 and 26:
Roger Vlitos; pages 13 and 22: Eye
Ubiquitous; page 24 top: Spectrum Colour
Library; page 24 bottom: Survival Anglia
Photo Library; pages 27 and 28-29: Frank
Spooner Pictures; page 28 top: Centre For
Alternative Technology Machynlleth,
Wales; page 28 bottom: Science Photo
Library; page 29 right: The Hutchison
Library.

INTRODUCTION

An environmentalist studies the Earth, climate and living creatures to understand the relationships between them. Today's environmentalists are also concerned with preserving nature, protecting animals and conserving the planet's resources. They hunt down and collect clues from the past and interpret existing life cycles to make predictions about the environment's future. Through fieldwork, mapping and observation they are helping piece together the world's most fascinating living puzzle – one that is changing more rapidly than ever before because of human influences.

This book is a practical guide to exploring the environment and an introduction to the environmentalist's science. Inside you will find experiments to help you investigate your surroundings and ideas for conservation at home and at school.

CONTENTS

OUR ENVIRONMENT

A picture of the Earth taken from space (photo left) shows land and sea, and swirling clouds. It gives clues about the climate in different parts of the Earth, which in turn determines the different habitats below. The temperature and the amount of rain affect what kind of plants will grow. If the right balance of sunlight, warmth, and moisture exists, plants will grow. Where rainfall is high and temperatures constant, as around the equator, great rainforests grow. Where it is too dry for trees, grasslands may still thrive. If it is very dry, as in the desert, little grows.

About 11 per cent of the Earth's land can be cultivated. By the year 2000 about half of this land will be farmed.

The natural habitats of the world are very varied. Some, like the rainforests, have been destroyed by humans. In other cases humans have altered landscapes and created artificial habitats which have much in common with natural habitats.

About two fifths of the land should be forest, but much has been cut down.

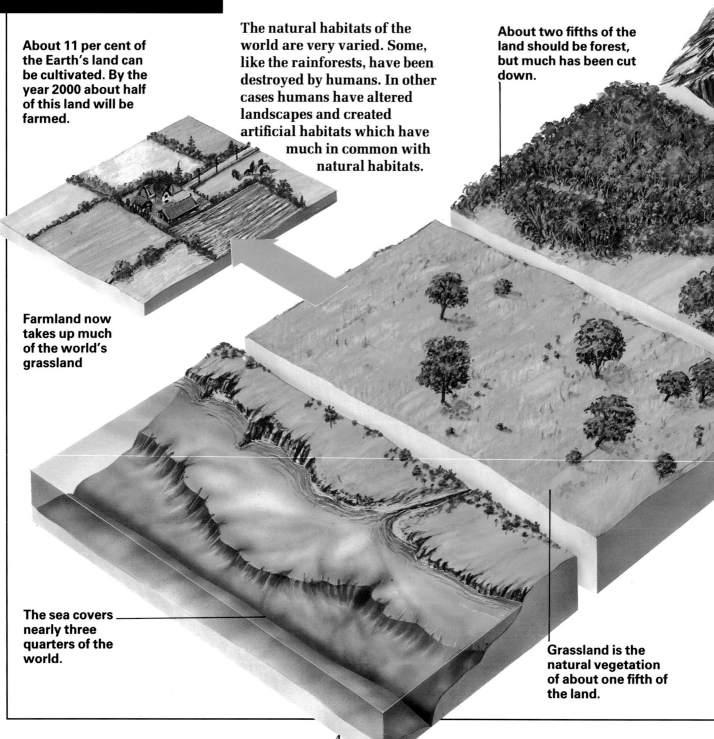

Farmland now takes up much of the world's grassland

The sea covers nearly three quarters of the world.

Grassland is the natural vegetation of about one fifth of the land.

4

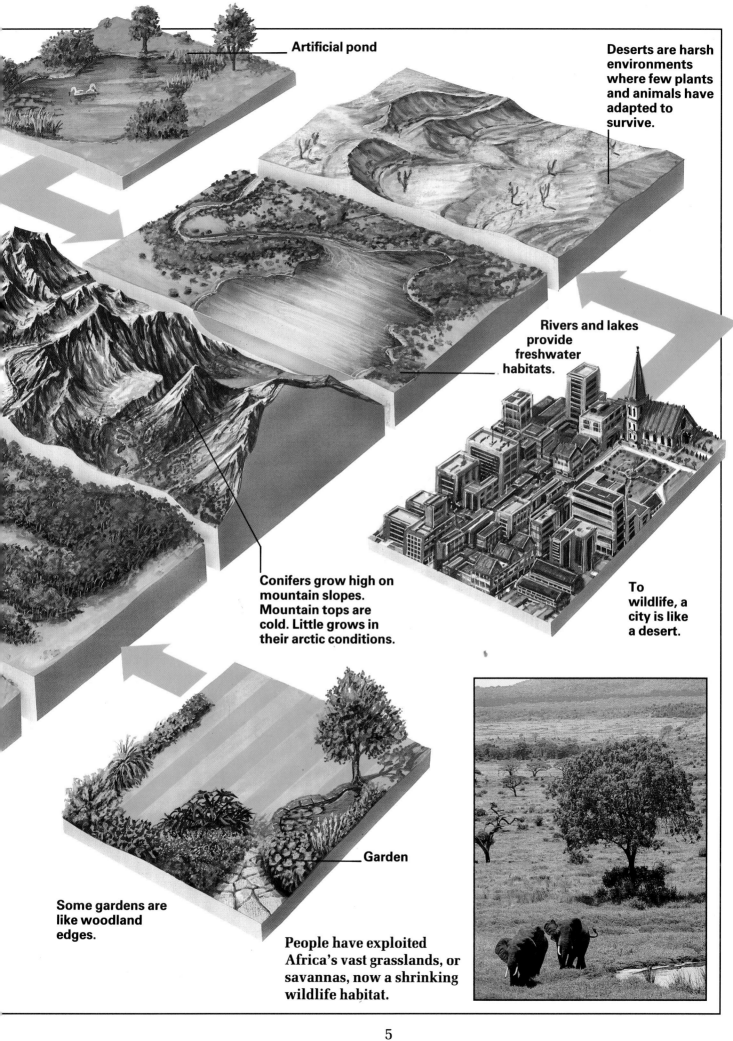

Artificial pond

Deserts are harsh environments where few plants and animals have adapted to survive.

Rivers and lakes provide freshwater habitats.

Conifers grow high on mountain slopes. Mountain tops are cold. Little grows in their arctic conditions.

To wildlife, a city is like a desert.

Garden

Some gardens are like woodland edges.

People have exploited Africa's vast grasslands, or savannas, now a shrinking wildlife habitat.

DELICATE BALANCE

The living world performs a delicate balancing act. Living things can only exist where conditions are right and depend on each other for survival. Only a few living things can survive without oxygen from the Earth's atmosphere. They all need water. They need the right climate and the right temperature, not too wet and not too dry, not too hot and not too cold. Above all, each living thing forms part of a system, depending on others for survival.

ECOSYSTEMS IN SCALE
Parrots in a rainforest and fish on a coral reef are part of different ecosystems. Taken together, creatures, plants and their habitat make an ecosystem. The largest ecosystems into which the Earth's land is divided are called biomes. For example, the tropical forest biome, which includes all tropical forests on every continent, takes up about one-fifth of all land. A community consists of the animals and plants in a small area. Within a community are populations, for example, all the rabbits in one wood.

Biome

Community

Two populations

6

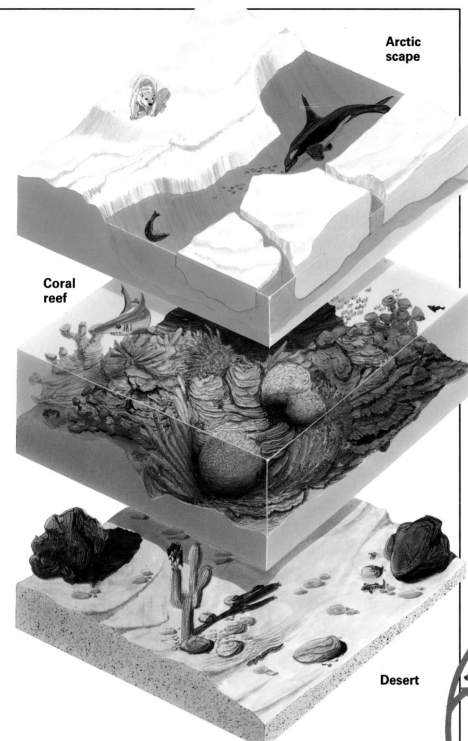

Arctic scape

Coral reef

Desert

FOOD WEBS

In a simple food chain an underwater plant makes its own food. A shrimp comes along and eats the plant. A fish eats the shrimp, which is eaten in turn by a seal. Later, a whale eats the seal. People catch and eat the whale. In fact, food chains are very rarely as simple as this. Most animals eat several different foods. Several other animals may eat them. Food chains are all interwoven, forming a food web, like the one shown below. These can sometimes be very complicated indeed. But they show how living things in an ecosystem depend on each other for survival.

FOOD WEBS

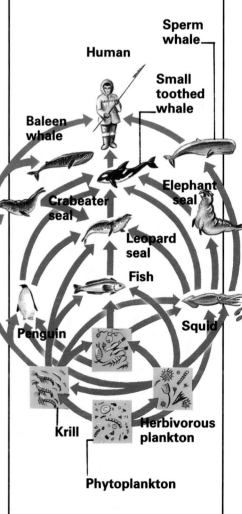

Sperm whale

Human

Small toothed whale

Baleen whale

Elephant seal

Crabeater seal

Leopard seal

Fish

Penguin

Squid

Krill

Herbivorous plankton

Phytoplankton

MAKING A LIVING

Some ecosystems are more complex than others. A desert has few kinds of animal and plant life. This is partly because conditions are so harsh. But there are also few ways of making a living here. In a tropical forest, on the other hand, there is a bounty of trees, flowers and other plants. Birds, monkeys, frogs, snakes and vast numbers of insects will all coexist.

The way that an animal makes its living is known as its "niche". Coral reefs, perhaps the oldest ecosystems, are teeming with niches. Taking up just a small space on the planet, they support one-third of all fish species. In the Arctic, where there are few niches, things look simpler. But even the simplest eco-system has a lot going on in it.

AIR AROUND US

The mixture of gases that surrounds us, sandwiched between the Earth and interplanetary space, is known as the atmosphere. The layer closest to the Earth's surface, the troposphere, extends an average of about ten kilometers. Above this the atmosphere becomes thinner and colder and fades into the space beyond.

Our weather is affected by air movements that take place in the troposphere. Air here contains water vapour, which creates the clouds that bring rain and snow. Dust specks in the atmosphere make spectacular red sunsets when they act as prisms to refract the Sun's rays.

AIR

Air is made of 78 per cent nitrogen gas, 21 per cent oxygen (O_2) and a small amount of argon and other gases. These other "trace" gases include neon, krypton, helium, methane and hydrogen. Carbon dioxide (CO_2) gas makes up only 0.034 per cent of the atmosphere, but its importance is tremendous: almost all the carbon in living things comes from this trace gas. The amount of each ingredient in the atmosphere is changing, altered both by the Earth's natural forces and the actions of people.

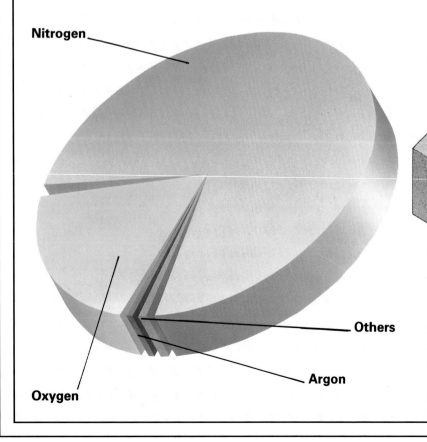

Nitrogen

Others

Argon

Oxygen

CARBON AND OXYGEN CYCLES

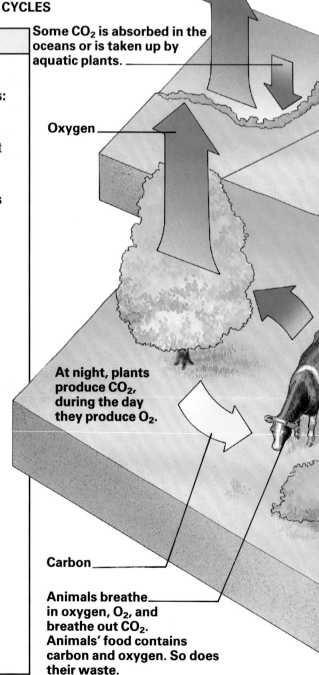

Some CO_2 is absorbed in the oceans or is taken up by aquatic plants.

Oxygen

At night, plants produce CO_2, during the day they produce O_2.

Carbon

Animals breathe in oxygen, O_2, and breathe out CO_2. Animals' food contains carbon and oxygen. So does their waste.

CYCLES

Atoms of elements such as carbon and oxygen are always being taken from the surroundings by living things. But they do not stay forever in animals or plants. They may be lost from them again through processes such as breathing, or upon death, to be taken up by the land, oceans and atmosphere. Elements are recycled, round and round through all of time.

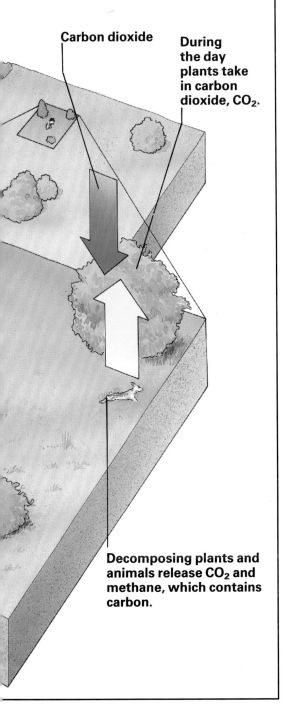

Carbon dioxide

During the day plants take in carbon dioxide, CO_2.

Decomposing plants and animals release CO_2 and methane, which contains carbon.

TRAPPING HEAT

Carbon dioxide is an important gas for life. Firstly, it provides a starting point for plants to make food. Secondly, it helps to warm the Earth. The Sun's rays strike the Earth, and heat its surface. Some heat is radiated back from the surface towards space. The small amount of carbon dioxide in the air acts like the glass in a greenhouse, stopping some heat radiation from escaping. This heat stays in the atmosphere and helps warm it, while some of the radiation is reflected back to Earth.

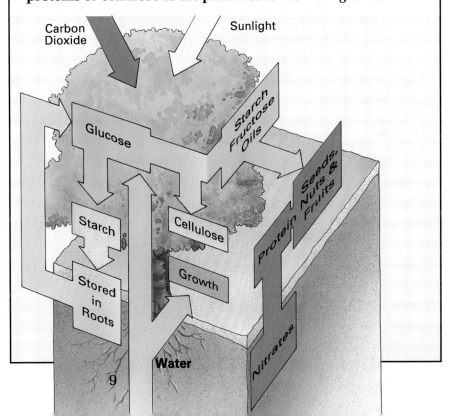

Sun rays

Carbon dioxide in the atmosphere traps the Sun's heat, warming the Earth.

Earth

PHOTOSYNTHESIS

When a plant photosynthesises, it uses energy from the Sun to convert carbon dioxide from the air and water from the soil to a simple sugar called glucose. This takes place in the leaves. The glucose can be further converted into starch, oil, proteins or cellulose as the plant needs them for growth.

Carbon Dioxide

Sunlight

Glucose

Starch
Fructose
Oils

Starch

Cellulose

Protein Seeds, Nuts & Fruits

Stored in Roots

Growth

Nitrates

Water

INVESTIGATING POLLUTION

Many human activities add substances to the air in such large amounts that they can be harmful and difficult to clear up. In other words, they cause pollution. Carried in the air, they may cause damage a long way from where they started. Coal-burning power stations release chemicals such as sulphur dioxide into the air. This substance combines with water vapour to produce damaging acids.

Nitrogen oxides are pumped into the air from power stations. Car exhausts contain them, too, together with lead compounds and carbon monoxide. Pesticides used by farmers to protect their crops can get into the air and be dispersed by the wind. All these things can act as poisons to humans and other living things.

Nitrous oxide

Chemicals (factories)

Pesticides

Carbon monoxide and dioxide (burning of fossil fuels)

LEAF WASHING

Hold a jar with water up to a leaf and wash both sides with a wet paintbrush. Save the dirty water. Repeat with nine more leaves, adding the dirt from each to your jar. Filter the water and inspect what is left on the filter paper. This is only the insoluble dirt in the air. Some polluting chemicals may have dissolved in the water. Now perform the same test on plants grown elsewhere, try one from near a railway and another from the seaside, for instance. Where is the air the cleanest?

Wash leaves with paint brush.

Pour water through filter paper in funnel.

Compare filter papers from different areas.

AIR TEST

Try setting a "trap" for the dirt floating in the air. With this experiment, you may even be able to tell whether the air is dirtier on some days than others. Find a wind-free spot outdoors. On a large sheet of white paper write the numbers 1 to 7. Write matching numbers on seven similar jar lids, and put them on "their" number. Leave the paper in position for a week. Each day remove a jar lid, starting with 1, finishing with 7. You will now have on your paper a daily pollution measure. Where is the paper dirtiest? Were there any days when a specially large amount of dirt was deposited? Record your results, repeat the test somewhere else and compare the results.

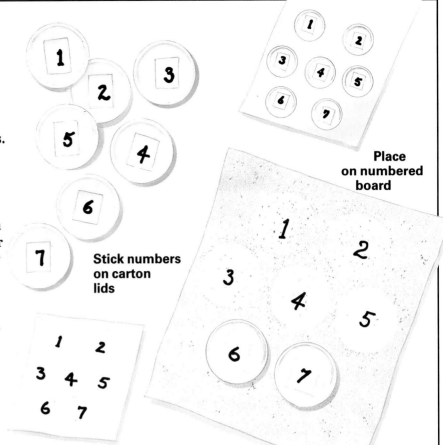

Stick numbers on carton lids

Place on numbered board

STUNTING GROWTH

Air pollution can drop chemicals onto the ground. These may contaminate the water that plants take into their roots. "Acid rain" (see page 15) is a serious problem in some places. You can investigate the effects of pollution on plants by growing cress and feeding it with contaminated water. Cress grows well on cotton wool or blotting paper.

Number your cress pots and put a matching number on some bottles for the water mixtures. You may collect your pollutants from the air or by leaf washing or using salt or soap and add each to a water bottle. Use ordinary water on one pot as a comparison. Sprinkle each pot with the matching numbered water mixture and watch and record what happens.

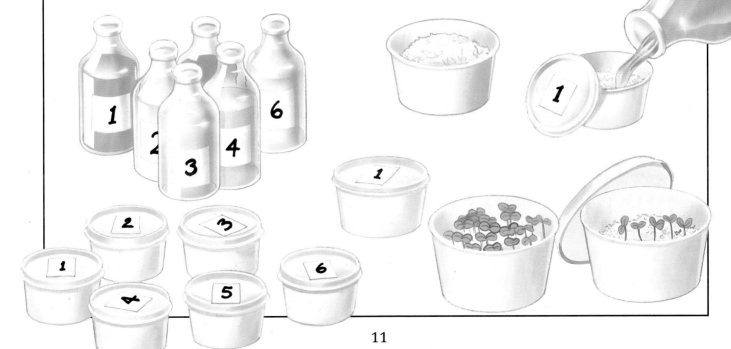

WATER FOR LIFE

Water is the stuff of life – the original home of all living things. Without it, plants and animals cannot function. Nature provides a constantly renewed source of fresh water for the land in the form of rain. Much of this water is returned to the oceans and cycles around again to be evaporated by the Sun. Solar energy performs a feat of awesome proportions, each year sucking up 400,000 cubic kilometres of water from oceans, rivers, lakes and streams. Nowadays people interfere in many ways with the supply and circulation of water. It is vitally important that we do not ruin the "water cycle". A supply of clean and uncontaminated water is necessary for survival.

IMPORTANT WATER

About 70% of the Earth's surface is covered by oceans. In addition there are many large lakes and rivers and innumerable smaller ponds and streams as shown above. These all provide important environments for living things. The "environment" inside us is also mainly water – about 70% of every adult and even more for some animals and plants.

70% of the Earth is covered in water.

Humans are made up of 70% water.

THE WATER CYCLE

Water evaporates from the sea. When it cools clouds form and from them rain falls. Rain seeps into the ground and runs off into waterways to evaporate once again. Plants take up water from the Earth and lose it as vapour through their pores. Animals lose water through respiration and waste. This water recycles too.

Clouds form

Respiration from living things

Evaporation from the ocean

Rain falls

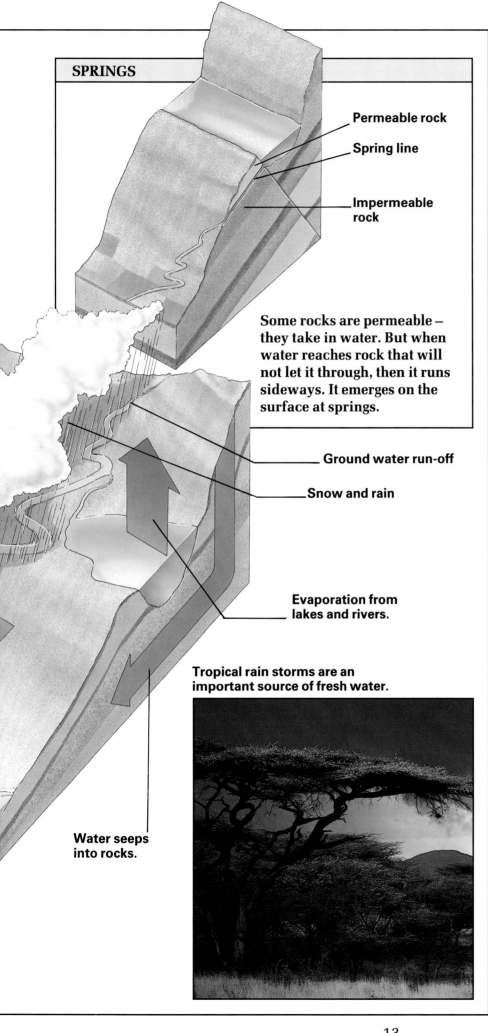

SPRINGS

Permeable rock

Spring line

Impermeable rock

Some rocks are permeable – they take in water. But when water reaches rock that will not let it through, then it runs sideways. It emerges on the surface at springs.

Ground water run-off

Snow and rain

Evaporation from lakes and rivers.

Tropical rain storms are an important source of fresh water.

Water seeps into rocks.

TYPES OF WATER

Fresh water contains few dissolved salts. The seas have many dissolved substances, especially "common salt", sodium chloride. Where a sea and river mix, you get brackish water.

Brackish

Fresh

Salt

MAKING A WATER CYCLE
Pour some water inside a large bowl and carefully place a small, empty bowl inside. Cover the large bowl with a sheet of cling film. Weight the middle of this cover over the inner bowl. Leave the bowl in the sun and watch your rain fall.

Weight   Polythene

Water collected in bowl

WATER POLLUTION

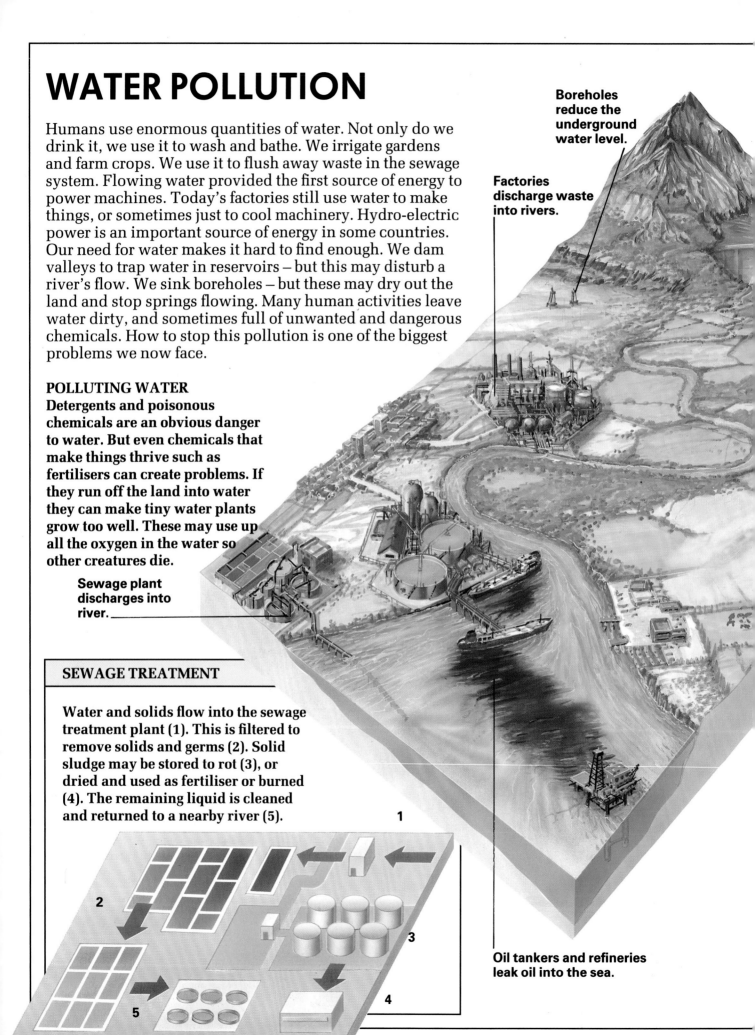

Humans use enormous quantities of water. Not only do we drink it, we use it to wash and bathe. We irrigate gardens and farm crops. We use it to flush away waste in the sewage system. Flowing water provided the first source of energy to power machines. Today's factories still use water to make things, or sometimes just to cool machinery. Hydro-electric power is an important source of energy in some countries. Our need for water makes it hard to find enough. We dam valleys to trap water in reservoirs – but this may disturb a river's flow. We sink boreholes – but these may dry out the land and stop springs flowing. Many human activities leave water dirty, and sometimes full of unwanted and dangerous chemicals. How to stop this pollution is one of the biggest problems we now face.

POLLUTING WATER

Detergents and poisonous chemicals are an obvious danger to water. But even chemicals that make things thrive such as fertilisers can create problems. If they run off the land into water they can make tiny water plants grow too well. These may use up all the oxygen in the water so other creatures die.

Sewage plant discharges into river.

SEWAGE TREATMENT

Water and solids flow into the sewage treatment plant (1). This is filtered to remove solids and germs (2). Solid sludge may be stored to rot (3), or dried and used as fertiliser or burned (4). The remaining liquid is cleaned and returned to a nearby river (5).

Boreholes reduce the underground water level.

Factories discharge waste into rivers.

Oil tankers and refineries leak oil into the sea.

1
2
3
4
5

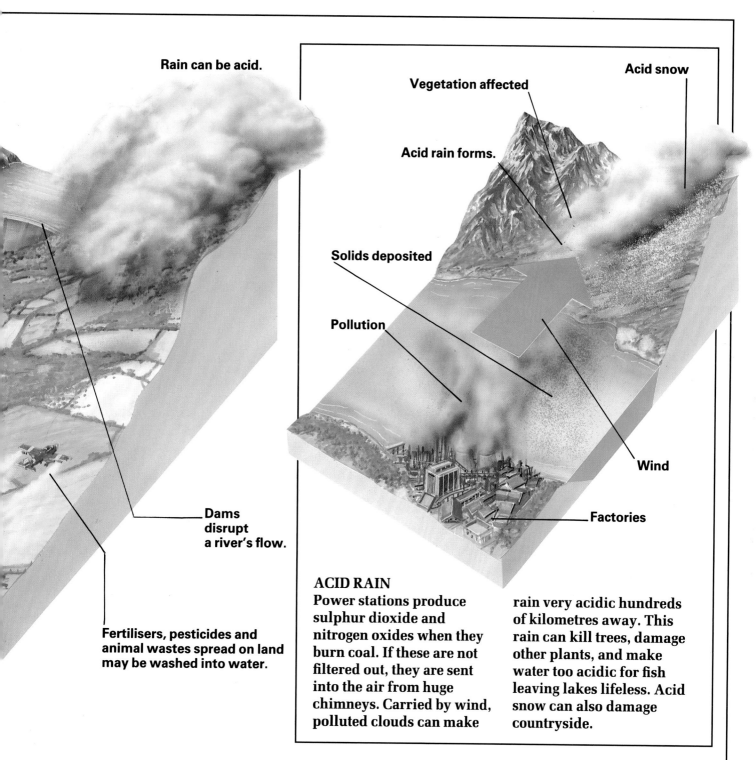

Rain can be acid.

Vegetation affected

Acid snow

Acid rain forms.

Solids deposited

Pollution

Wind

Dams disrupt a river's flow.

Factories

Fertilisers, pesticides and animal wastes spread on land may be washed into water.

ACID RAIN
Power stations produce sulphur dioxide and nitrogen oxides when they burn coal. If these are not filtered out, they are sent into the air from huge chimneys. Carried by wind, polluted clouds can make rain very acidic hundreds of kilometres away. This rain can kill trees, damage other plants, and make water too acidic for fish leaving lakes lifeless. Acid snow can also damage countryside.

DANGER IN THE FOOD CHAIN
Some substances that are used to control pests break down soon after they are used. But some do not, and these may be passed up the food chain to animals which are not the original target of the poison. The poison may build up to harmful levels in animals at the top of the chain.

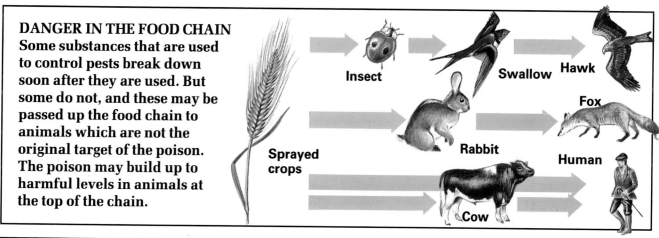

Insect   Swallow   Hawk

Fox

Sprayed crops   Rabbit

Human

Cow

THE ACID TEST

Environmentalists test for acid in rain and snow. You can measure how acidic a solution is using an indicator paper. Some kinds, such as litmus paper, can be bought. But you can make your own using the dye that gives red cabbage its colour. Find out how the paper's colour changes with acidity by making solutions with varying amounts of acid in them, by mixing a solution of vinegar and water. Then find out how acidic your rain is by comparison.

Chop up a red cabbage and pour on hot water.

Leave to soak.

Pour cabbage water through sieve.

Dip strips of blotting paper in the cabbage water, then leave to dry.

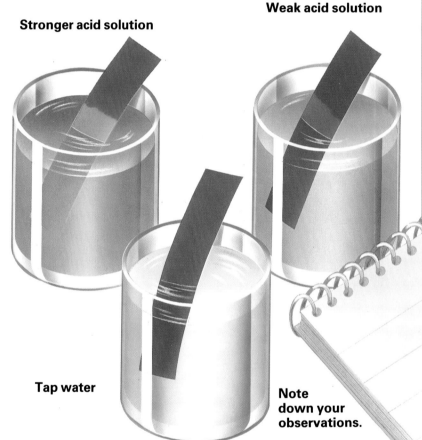

Stronger acid solution

Weak acid solution

Tap water

Note down your observations.

ACID WATCH

By sampling rain you can discover if it seems to be more acidic than it should be. Collect it as it falls in a clean, dry vessel, to avoid contaminating the sample. Test rainfall from different neighbourhoods and at different times of year using the method described above. Make observations about the location – are there power stations nearby? Do buildings and statues appear to have been damaged by acid?

You may also be able to collect water samples from local lakes or streams and test their acidity. If they are acid, this may have come from a source other than rain. Can you find out what it may be?

EATEN BY ACID

If you want to see how acid water affects plants, you can do your own experiment. Use plants such as beans, which grow fast. Once they are growing, make three watering bottles, one with water, one made slightly acid with vinegar, another very acid. Observe how the plants grow once you start using these solutions to water them.

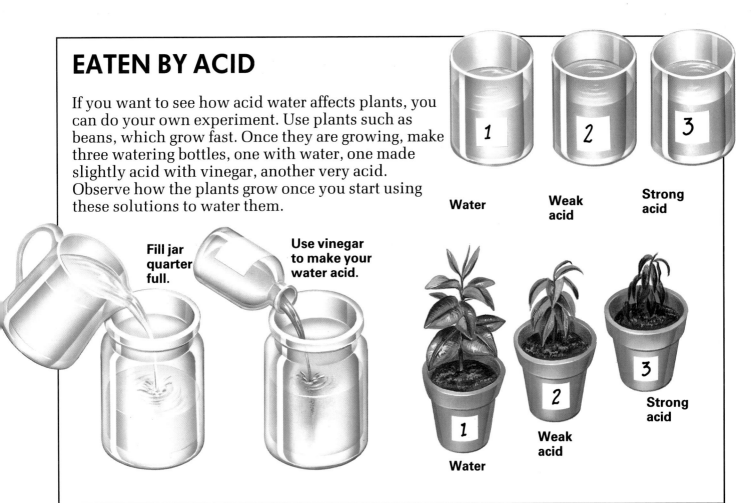

Water

Weak acid

Strong acid

Fill jar quarter full.

Use vinegar to make your water acid.

Strong acid

Weak acid

Water

FILTERING

Filtration helps to purify water. Treatment plants sieve the water to remove algae. Often the sand particles are filtered out. Germ-killing chlorine is added in a final stage before the clean water is pumped through our pipes.

Try filtering water yourself to see how well it works. First, make something to filter! Stir soil, leaves, grass and other garden refuse together to make very dirty water indeed. Pour it through a filter in the bottom of a flowerpot, and see what comes through. Try several filter materials such as gravel, cloth, or blotting paper, to see which does the job best. Filtering will not remove chemicals that dissolve in water, so do not drink your "clean" water.

Mix soil, leaves and other debris with some water.

Make a blotting paper filter the right size for your pot.

Pour through your mixture.

INVESTING IN LAND

Ever since the earliest farmers thousands of years ago, humans have used land for agriculture. Now large parts of the world are no longer truly wild, but have been settled and turned into farmland as the picture on the left shows. As well as farming, we develop the land in many other ways. We build towns and cities, and the roads that connect them. We use areas for sport and recreation. Used sensitively, the land can support farming and much wildlife too, but if the land and soils are treated badly, then both farming and wildlife suffer. We have to remember that we must eat, and we can only feed ourselves if the land is kept in good health.

TESTING SOIL

You can find the things that make up your soil. Simply take a soil sample and place it in a jam jar. Cover it with plenty of water and put the lid on. Shake vigorously for a while, and the soil will be suspended in water. Now all you have to do is leave the jar, preferably for a few days. You can then see what has settled out. The densest or biggest pieces settle first, the fine ones last. Humus and dead leaves may float. How much of your soil is pebble, sand or clay? Has it got plenty of humus? Test several different soils.

Jam jar with soil sample.

Cover with water.

Put lid on and shake well.

Leave to settle.

1   2   3

Small farms are often more productive for each unit of area than large ones.

Soil is formed by the effects of weather on rocks at the Earth's surface. Depending on how small the rock particles are, the soil may be gravel, sand or clay and also contain other minerals. Mixed in with this may be humus, the remains of plants. Soil also contains bacteria, small animals, water and air. The mixture determines which plants grow, and how well.

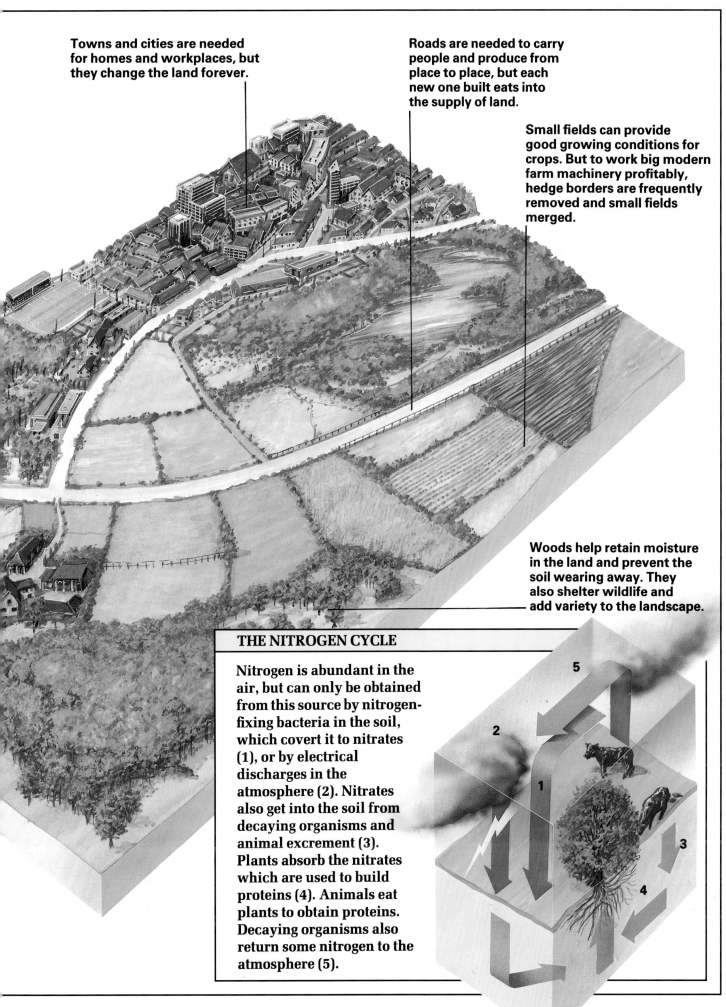

Towns and cities are needed for homes and workplaces, but they change the land forever.

Roads are needed to carry people and produce from place to place, but each new one built eats into the supply of land.

Small fields can provide good growing conditions for crops. But to work big modern farm machinery profitably, hedge borders are frequently removed and small fields merged.

Woods help retain moisture in the land and prevent the soil wearing away. They also shelter wildlife and add variety to the landscape.

THE NITROGEN CYCLE

Nitrogen is abundant in the air, but can only be obtained from this source by nitrogen-fixing bacteria in the soil, which covert it to nitrates (1), or by electrical discharges in the atmosphere (2). Nitrates also get into the soil from decaying organisms and animal excrement (3). Plants absorb the nitrates which are used to build proteins (4). Animals eat plants to obtain proteins. Decaying organisms also return some nitrogen to the atmosphere (5).

DISAPPEARING LAND

There is much less land than there was. The ground beneath is still there, of course, but in many parts of the world, wild places are now being taken over for farms. In some parts, such as western Europe, this process has been going on for so long that there are few places that have not been altered by people. There may come a time in the next century when there is nowhere on Earth untouched by humans. But the story does not end here. Farmland itself is under threat from the spread of cities. In some places farmland has been overworked, with people trying to grow too many crops or keep too many cattle. Overuse can destroy soil. During a drought, overused soil may turn to desert.

Since the 1920's cities have been spreading rapidly to make room for more people. With motor cars, people no longer need to live close to their work. They may also like houses with gardens. All this adds to the size of cities.

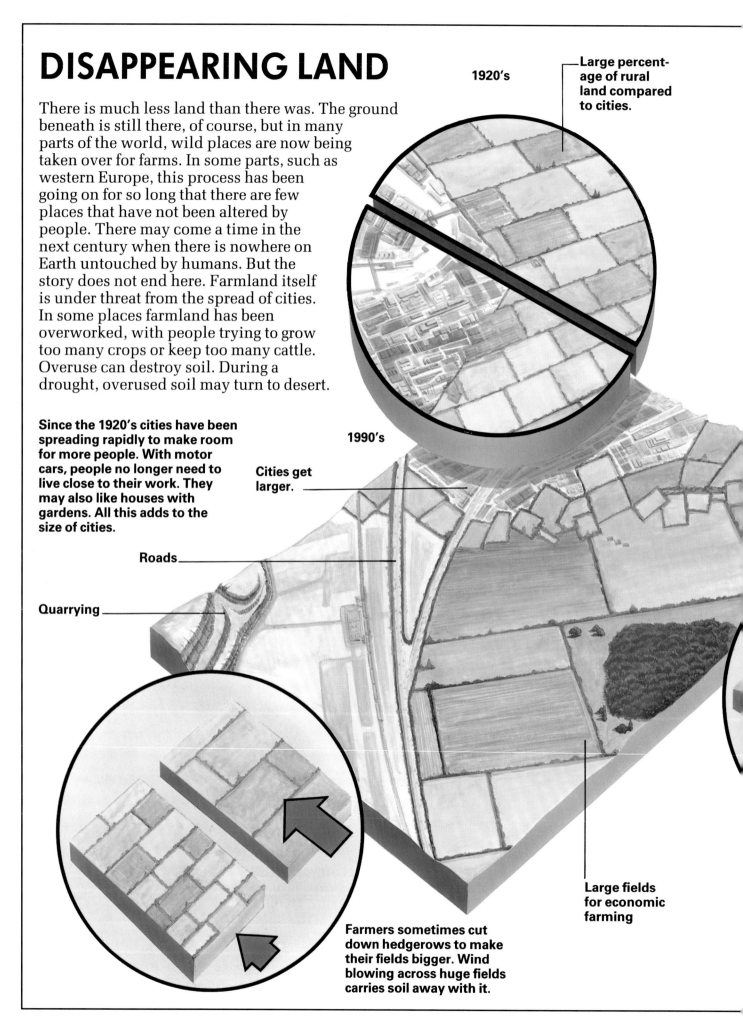

1920's

Large percentage of rural land compared to cities.

1990's

Cities get larger.

Roads

Quarrying

Large fields for economic farming

Farmers sometimes cut down hedgerows to make their fields bigger. Wind blowing across huge fields carries soil away with it.

With more machinery, fewer people need to work on farms. They leave the country for the cities to look for a living. This adds to crowded city populations. Cities spread even more. Golf courses and sports facilities may improve city life but they also take up precious land.

Quarrying may spoil and pollute, but usually the damage is often local and there is a chance it can be repaired. The damage done by spreading housing, roads, farming and grazing is often slower and less dramatic. But it may be more permanent and dangerous in the long run.

Woods and forests are destroyed to make way for farming or building.

More and more people own motor cars and want to drive from place to place. New roads and motorways are built to make travel easier. But these can take up huge areas of land that might otherwise be productive.

RAINFOREST DESTRUCTION

Each minute of every day, an area of rainforest the size of 60 football pitches is felled. At this rate the rainforests will disappear in 50 years. This leads to extensive soil erosion as farms built on the cleared land rapidly exhaust the poor soil of its nutrients.

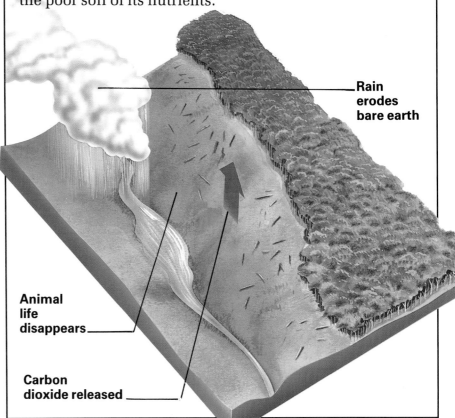

Rain erodes bare earth

Animal life disappears

Carbon dioxide released

LANDFILL

Thousands of tonnes of rubbish need to be disposed of every day. The waste is often put into holes in the ground, using old quarries or valleys. Covered by a layer of earth, a landfill can then be planted and landscaped. But sometimes buried rubbish hides problems which may remain underground. Methane from decomposing rubbish can bubble up while dangerous waste releases harmful toxins into soil and water.

Layers of soil

Rubbish

TAKE A LOOK AROUND

How does your own area of the world look? Does it look like the picture on the left? What is the land used for around you? Does it provide a good home for animal and plant life? Or is it a wildlife desert? Could it be made better? These are just some of the questions you may be able to answer if you make an expedition around your home town. Whether you live in a big city, or in the country, you can find out what is going on in the environment around you by exploring and recording what you see.

Explore the streets and open areas around your home.

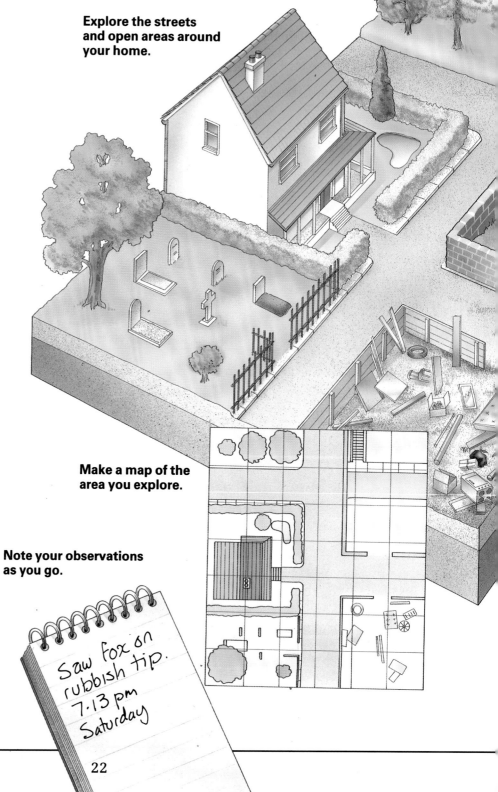

Make a map of the area you explore.

Note your observations as you go.

Saw fox on rubbish tip. 7.13 pm Saturday

LICHEN TEST

Lichens are strange plants, a combination of a fungus and an alga. Different kinds are able to withstand different amounts of pollution. For a gauge of local pollution, note the lichens around you and in other areas.

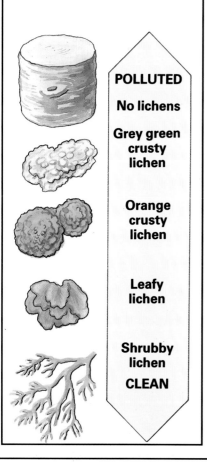

POLLUTED

No lichens

Grey green crusty lichen

Orange crusty lichen

Leafy lichen

Shrubby lichen

CLEAN

WASTE

On the whole, the richer a country, the more waste it produces. People in rich western countries throw away many things that would be used again in poorer countries. Our waste includes items from vegetable peelings to scrap cars. Much waste nowadays comes from packaging materials. Some waste is easy to break down and reuse. For example, vegetable scraps can be used on a garden compost heap. Some scrap metal, and even plastics, can be melted down and used again. So can a lot of paper. But there are some plastics and other materials that cannot be recycled. These add to the problem of waste disposal.

TYPES OF RUBBISH

Glass

Tin

Paper

Natural

Material

Plastic

Rotting
Natural materials such as plant and animal remains are soon broken down by bacteria and fungi. This picture shows an avocado at various stages of decay.

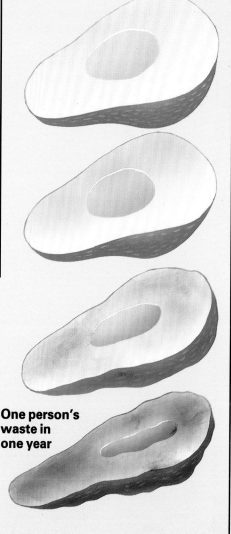

One person's waste in one year

CLIMATE CHANGE

Weather changes from day to day, season to season and even over longer periods of time. The climate of a region may change altogether. For example, the Sahara used to be a grassland thousands of years ago. Now it's a desert. Because of the pollution we continually pump into the atmosphere, we could be drastically changing the atmosphere ourselves. Recent winters in the Alps have seen many places without their usual cover of snow. This could be a sign of climatic change.

THE GREENHOUSE EFFECT
The amount of carbon dioxide in the atmosphere has increased slightly in the last 100 years. It is believed this increase is caused by the burning of fossil fuels and destruction of rainforests. If the build-up continues, more heat will be trapped in the atmosphere and an increase in the average temperature over the Earth may occur (global warming).

ICE AGES

There have been several Ice Ages when the climate of the Earth was colder than average. Ice that spread from the poles and glaciers covered much of Europe and North America. The last Ice Age ended 10,000 years ago. Some scientists think that the world is returning to an Ice Age climate. But more people fear global warming.

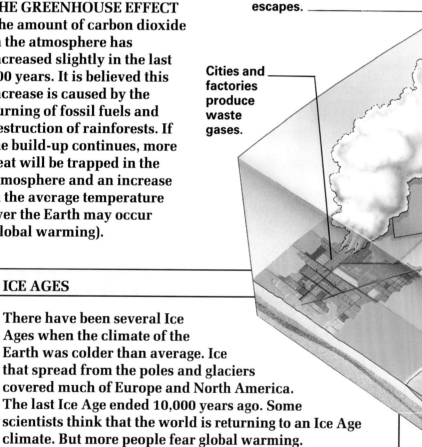

Some heat escapes.

Cities and factories produce waste gases.

Heat is reflected back towards the Earth.

Heat radiation from the Sun

CFCs

CFCs are chemicals used in aerosol cans, refrigerators and in making polystyrene. If released into the air, they break down when exposed to ultraviolet light, giving off chlorine. The danger is that this chlorine may attack the ozone that forms a protective layer from ultraviolet radiation in the atmosphere. Already, environmentalists have detected ozone damage.

Rainforest destruction

WEATHER WATCH

You can keep tabs on the weather in your area. You can make a rain gauge and measure how much falls each day. You can record wind direction, either with a weather vane or a wind sock. You may be able to estimate wind speeds too. How damp is the atmosphere? You can get complicated instruments to measure this, or you could just use an old pine cone, and notice whether it is open (dry) or closed (damp). Measure the temperature, too. Put the thermometer in the open but in the shade. You could make a chart of temperature and rainfall for each month. You would need to keep up your record for a long time, though, before you could even begin to guess whether the climate was changing!

Homemade rain gauge made from a plastic bottle that has the top cut off and sitting upside down in the base.

Make a card for each month and measure temperature, rainfall and record other observations such as animals seen or trees.

Take average rainfall and temperature and make graphs for each. Use symbols for such things as falling leaves.

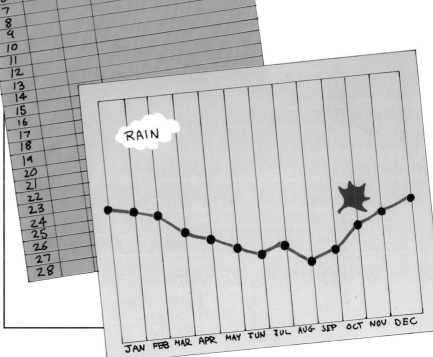

FEBRUARY

DATE	TEMP.	RAIN	OBSERVATIONS
1	8°C	0	FRESH, CLEAR DAY
2	9°C	0	CLOUDY DAY
3	8°C	1mm	BLUSTERY, RAINY
4	7°C	0	COLD, CLEAR DAY. BULBS
5			
6			
7			
8			
9			
10			
11			
12			
13			
14			
15			
16			
17			
18			
19			
20			
21			
22			
23			
24			
25			
26			
27			
28			

RAIN

JAN FEB MAR APR MAY JUN JUL AUG SEP OCT NOV DEC

TAKING ACTION

Faced with so many problems affecting the planet and threatening the environment, it could be easy to despair. But by taking action, you can both help save the Earth and feel less helpless. There is much we can do to put things right in our own home. It is essential that we look at ways of reducing the valuable resources we consume and throw away on a daily basis. Conserving energy at home, using more efficient electric appliances, and recycling wherever possible (see photo on the left of paper recycling) will start your contribution to the environment.

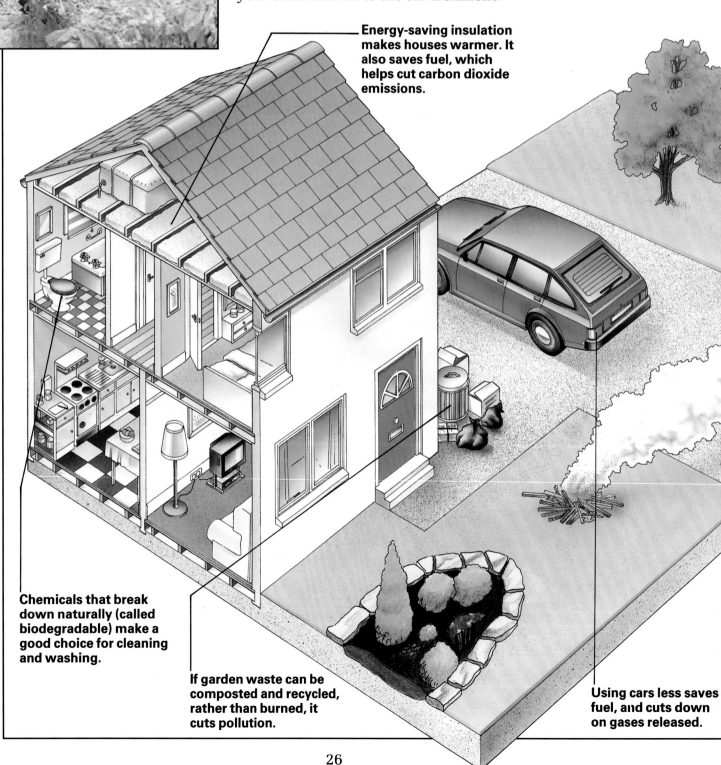

Energy-saving insulation makes houses warmer. It also saves fuel, which helps cut carbon dioxide emissions.

Chemicals that break down naturally (called biodegradable) make a good choice for cleaning and washing.

If garden waste can be composted and recycled, rather than burned, it cuts pollution.

Using cars less saves fuel, and cuts down on gases released.

What can you do?
Cut down on anything that wastes energy. Walk or cycle rather than take a car. Choose biodegradable products, or those which use renewable resources. Avoid aerosols containing CFCs. If possible, avoid products which use large amounts of packaging, especially if they cannot easily be recycled. If you have finished using something – a toy, some clothes, a bed – pass it on if you can rather than throw it away.

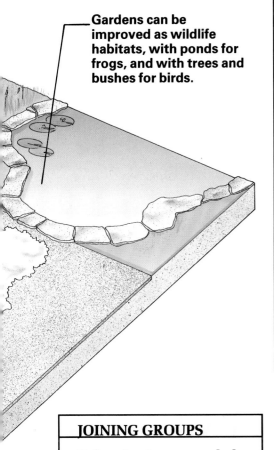

Gardens can be improved as wildlife habitats, with ponds for frogs, and with trees and bushes for birds.

JOINING GROUPS

Belonging to a group helps you get more information about what is happening in the environment. You can also join with other people to do something to help. Many areas have local conservation groups. There are also worldwide organisations, for you to join.

RECYCLING

Find out about any recycling schemes near you. Glass, metals, paper and even cloth can all be recycled. You may have a bottle bank near you for used glass bottles and jars, to be melted down and reused. There are sometimes similar banks for cans and tins. Paper can also be recycled. Many groups collect newspapers, which helps tree conservation.

POSTERS

If you know of a good recycling scheme you may like to publicise it. Or you may want to share your worries about the rubbish piling up in your neighbourhood, proposals to build a new road or fill a pond.Making a poster is an eye-catching and fun way of making your point, and letting other people know what is going on. Perhaps your school has a place to display posters.

SAVE OUR EARTH

THE FUTURE

By the end of this decade, the spread of towns, erosion, desertification and poisoning could cut the world's farmland by one-fifth of its 1975 level. The planet's wildlife is also under threat. More than 100 species of animals and birds have become extinct this century. If tropical forests are cut down, thousands more animals and plants will become extinct. Other habitats, from wetlands to savannas, are threatened. There is only a limited amount of fuel in the world. Known reserves of fossil fuels such as coal and oil are not expected to last beyond the next century.

KEEPING TREES

Wood is used as a fuel in much of the world, but the demand for wood leads to the chopping down of too many trees. Removing trees can expose soil to erosion creating deserts which are useless for farming. It is important to replant our trees for the future.

OZONE DEPLETION

A "hole" appears to be growing in the ozone layer over the poles. As a result, scientists believe that too many dangerous rays from the Sun are piercing through to Earth, and causing skin cancers as in the photo below.

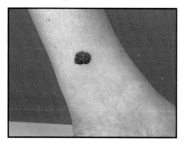

GREENHOUSE EFFECT

To cut the build-up of carbon dioxide in the atmosphere we may need to find ways of getting energy without burning fuels. Wind or wave energy may be harnessed successfully.

HABITAT DESTRUCTION

We need to halt the spread of deserts. Irrigation may be an answer, although in some places it has made ground too salty for crops. We need to replace forests. They can bind the soil, retain moisture and soak up carbon dioxide. Wetlands should be cherished, not drained.

NATURAL RESOURCES

The aim should be to use only what can be replaced. We should take no more wood from forests each year than can be reforested. We should use no more water than is replaced by rain. If we exceed this ration, then the world is bound to have a shortage of natural resources.

PEOPLE AND PLANET

Most of the problems we have looked at in this book can be summed up in one word – people. Long ago, when people were rare animals that lived in small bands, hunting and gathering the food they required, there were so few of us we made little impact on the world. Now we number more than five thousand million (5,000,000,000) and our impact on the environment is enormous. Some scientists think that our population, which is still growing, may level off at seven to ten billion some time next century. Others are not so sure. What is certain is that in some places it is already difficult to find enough food for everyone to eat. On the other hand, with careful and sensible use of land, it is almost certain that a world population larger than at present could be fed satisfactorily. It is really up to us: use the world wisely, and thrive, or ruin it, and suffer the consequences.

KEEPING RECORDS

An important part of being an environmentalist is keeping some sort of record of what you see and find out. Your observations will be more interesting to you, and more valuable to others, if they are carefully recorded. You may want to make records of pollution that you find, or to record how well an area is growing after being cleaned up. Carry a small notebook to jot down what you see. If you can, take photographs of scenes or details that may be important. You will find that in your memory, details are gradually forgotten. Records made at the time on paper or by camera are more reliable. If you want to encourage others to share your point of view, you will find that well-recorded facts are more convincing than hearsay.

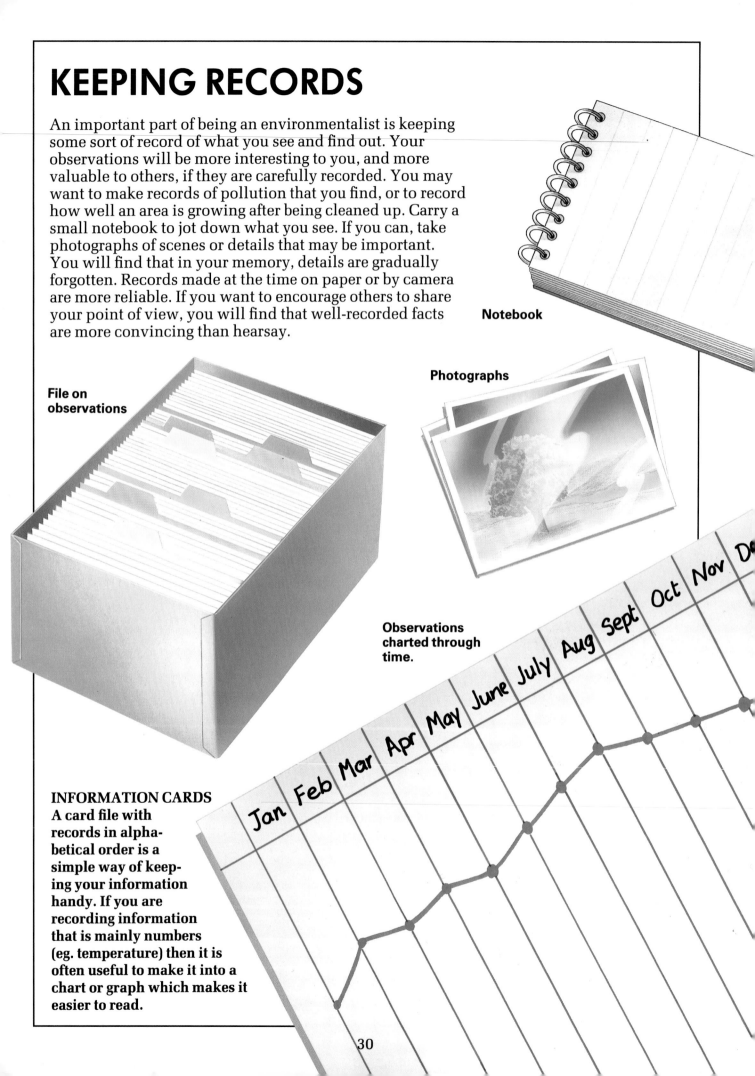

Notebook

File on observations

Photographs

Observations charted through time.

INFORMATION CARDS
A card file with records in alphabetical order is a simple way of keeping your information handy. If you are recording information that is mainly numbers (eg. temperature) then it is often useful to make it into a chart or graph which makes it easier to read.

Jan Feb Mar Apr May June July Aug Sept Oct Nov D

EQUIPMENT

The most important equipment you carry is your own senses. Your nose, eyes and ears are designed for telling you about your environment. A camera is good for recording what you see. Jars and plastic bags or boxes are good for specimens that you wish to take away. (Remember not to spoil your environment by overdoing this. Collecting some animals and plants is illegal – check what the regulations are first.) The garden variety experiments in this book will help you discover more about your environment, helping you to treat it more thoughtfully.

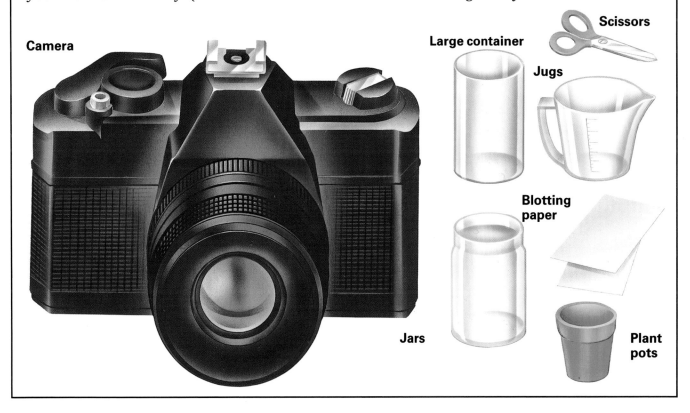

Camera

Large container

Scissors

Jugs

Blotting paper

Jars

Plant pots

ADDRESSES

The World-Wide Fund for Nature aims to protect habitats and wildlife.

WWF, Panda House, Weyside Park, Godalming, Surrey GU7 1XR

WWF, Level 17, St Martin's Tower, 31 Market Street, GPO Box 528, Sydney NSW 2001, Australia

Friends of the Earth is an organisation that campaigns for habitats.

FoE, 26-28 Underwood Street, London N1 7JQ

FoE, 366 Smith Street, Collingwood, VIC 3066, Australia

Greenpeace uses direct action to challenge environmental issues.

Greenpeace, 30-31 Islington Green, London N1 8XE
Greenpeace, 134 Broadway, NSW 2007, Australia.

Oxfam tries to improve conditions for humans in poor countries.

Oxfam, 274 Banbury Road, Oxford OX2 7DZ.

The British Trust for Conservation Volunteers concentrates on local practical projects.

BTCV, 36 St Mary's Street, Wallingford, Oxon OX10 0EU

GLOSSARY

acid rain rain made acid by the products from industry

atmosphere the gases that surround the Earth

biodegradable breaking down naturally, for example by the action of bacteria

biome a major world habitat, such as tropical forest

CFCs (chlorofluorocarbons) chemicals which may pose a threat to the ozone layer

community a collection of animals and plants of different kinds sharing the same habitat

conservation sensible and careful use of the environment

to avoid damage

ecosystem all the living organisms and their surroundings, within a defined area

environment the surroundings of a living thing, including other living things.

erosion the wearing away of rocks or soil by wind and water

food chain the "chain" of living things through which energy is passed, one feeding on the next

fossil fuel fuel such as oil or gas formed in the rocks from the bodies of dead organisms

global warming a suggested general warming of the Earth

through an increased greenhouse effect

habitat a certain area inhabited by animals and plants

niche the particular way in which an animal or plant "makes a living"

pesticides chemicals designed to kill pests

photosynthesis the process by which plants harness sunlight to make sugars

pollution spoiling of a habitat, especially as a result of human actions

troposphere the lower layer of the atmosphere

INDEX